Should Henry Wear a Helmet?

Staying Safe

Rebecca Rissman

Heinemann
LIBRARY

Chicago, Illinois

© 2013 Heinemann Library
an imprint of Capstone Global Library, LLC
Chicago, Illinois

To contact Capstone Global Library please phone 800-747-4992, or visit
our website www.capstonepub.com

Edited by Daniel Nunn, Rebecca Rissman, and Siân Smith
Designed by Steve Mead
Picture research by Mica Brancic
Production by Alison Parsons
Originated by Capstone Global Library Ltd
Printed and bound in China by Leo Paper Products Ltd

16 15 14 13 12
10 9 8 7 6 5 4 3 2 1

Library of Congress Cataloging-in-Publication Data
Rissman, Rebecca.
  Should henry wear a helmet? : staying safe / Rebecca Rissman.
    p. cm.—(What would you do?)
  Includes bibliographical references and index.
  ISBN 978-1-4329-7241-7 (hb)—ISBN 978-1-4329-7247-9 (pb) 1. Safety
education—Juvenile literature. 2. Accidents—Prevention—Juvenile
literature. I. Title.
  HQ770.7.R57 2013
  613.6—dc23   2012017435

Acknowledgments
All photographs © Capstone Publishers (Karon Dubke).

Every effort has been made to contact copyright holders of any material
reproduced in this book. Any omissions will be rectified in subsequent
printings if notice is given to the publisher.

Contents

Making Choices

We make choices every day, such as "Should I wear an apron?"

Our choices have effects.

Ask yourself if your choices will have good or bad effects.

Should Henry Wear a Helmet?

Henry wants to ride his bike. Should Henry wear a helmet?

Henry could choose to wear
his helmet.

Henry could choose not to wear
his helmet.

What Would YOU Have Done?

If Henry had worn his helmet, he would have stayed safe while riding his bike. If Henry had not worn his helmet and then fell off his bike, he could have been seriously hurt.

Should Billy Look Both Ways?

Billy is crossing the street. Should he look both ways before he crosses?

Billy could choose to look both ways.

Billy could choose not to look
both ways.

What Would YOU Have Done?

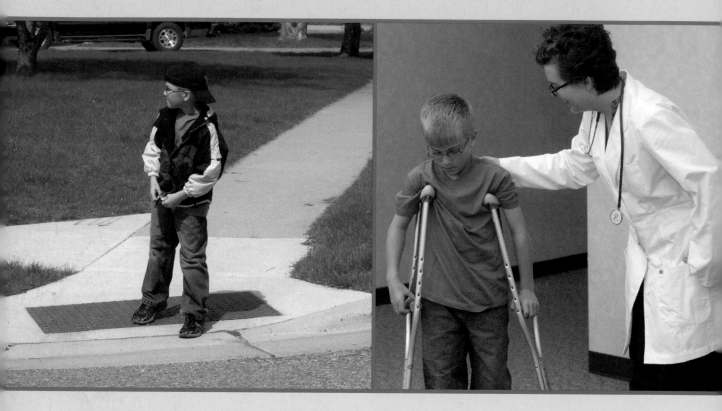

If Billy had looked both ways, he would have seen if any cars were coming. If Billy had not looked both ways, he might have been hit by a car.

Should Bella Wear Her Seat Belt?

Bella is going for a ride in a car.

Should Bella wear her seat belt?

Bella could choose to wear her seat belt.

Bella could choose not to wear her seat belt.

What Would YOU Have Done?

If Bella had worn a seat belt, she would have stayed safe in the car. If Bella had not worn a seat belt, she could have been hurt if the car had gotten into an accident.

Should Charlotte Help?

Charlotte's aunt has left the kitchen. Should Charlotte help her to cook while she's gone?

Charlotte could choose to cook alone.

Charlotte could choose to wait for her aunt to return.

What Would YOU Have Done?

If Charlotte had tried to help on her own, without asking first, she might have put herself in danger and could have had an accident. If she had waited for her aunt, they could have worked out the best way for her to help together.

Picture Glossary

accident something that happens by mistake

choice a decision

effects the results of a decision or something you choose to do. Choices can have good or bad effects.

helmet hard hat that protects your head

Index

Notes for Parents and Teachers
Before reading
Engage children in a discussion about making decisions. Ask children to explain how they make decisions. Ask children to reflect on a decision they made recently. Was the outcome good or bad? Could they have made a better decision?

After reading
In pairs, ask children to act out a scenario from the book. Each child can act out a different decision and outcome. Afterward, encourage children to discuss why one outcome was better than the other.